"There's just one more thing, Marilla.... Mrs. Barry told Diana that we might sleep in the spare-room bed. Think of the honour of your little Anne being put in the spare room bed."

Anne of Green Gables, L.M. Montgomery

Table of Contents

Introduction	pg. 04
Chapter 1: Clean Your House	pg. 05
Chapter 2: Call Pest Control	pg. 09
Chapter 3: Wash Your Linens	pg. 11
Chapter 4: Make Room	pg. 13
Chapter 5: Provide Toiletries	pg. 17
Chapter 6: Feed Them	pg. 20
Chapter 7: Provide a Peaceful Atmosphere	pg. 22
Chapter 8: Maintain a Fragrant Environment	pg. 23
Chapter 9: Control Your Pets...And Theirs	pg. 25
Chapter 10: Coordinate Your Schedules	pg. 27
Chapter 11: Provide Them with a List of Nearby Necessities, Food & Fun	pg. 28
Chapter 12: Clearly Communicate	pg. 30
BONUS: How to Setup a Guest Room	pg. 33
Contact	pg. 51

Introduction

I am 32 years old and in my short life, I have experienced a vast array of hosting experiences including everything from clean, calming environments to things not lawful to be uttered. (If only you knew...the utter and absolute horror!) I've always been a lifestyle buff for most of my life and even had an award-winning wedding blog (daweddings.wordpress.com) as well as a lifestyle blog (thehostesslist.wordpress.com) for a while, so I wanted to take a moment to discuss the natural as well as the practical when it comes to hosting overnight guests in your home.

  Now, some of you (many I hope) will think some or even many of these points are common sensical, and they are! Yet I have been forced to realise that everybody was either not taught the same way, not taught at all, or simply does not realise that their hosting abilities could stand to be improved. So if this is an education to you, I'm happy to provide it! And if this is a refresher course, I hope it's a blessing to you as well, and something that you'll share with others. Now, let's go!

Chapter 1: Clean Your House

CLEAN.YOUR.HOUSE. Clean the living and dining areas. Clean the kitchen. Clean the bathrooms. Clean the rooms, especially the ones your guest(s) will be occupying...clean everything. And if you simply don't have the time or ability to do it, then hire someone to do it for you (even your kids). Place special emphasis on the bathrooms. There is nothing like going into a room where you're supposed to be clean, but feeling dirty because the bathroom itself is dirty.

Things Not Lawful to be Uttered...

The aforementioned "things not lawful to be uttered" that I've seen and experienced fell 1,000% into this category. I will not give you all of the dirty details (see "not lawful to be uttered"), but suffice it to say, on a recent trip, my friends and I arrived at the intended home, no hosts present on this trip (which was expected), and were welcomed with, well, things not lawful to be uttered. So instead of relaxing and settling in at 1 in the morning, three out of the four of us began to deep clean this house top to bottom in an attempt to make it even the slightest bit tolerable.

Okay, I'm being a bit dramatic. But had you seen the foul state of the ENTIRE house, then you may very well have felt the same dramatic feelings we did. I've yet to see anything worse in all my days, except for on episodes of TLC's *Hoarders*. That said, here are some of the mild-to-horrific things I've experienced over the years:

- No towels
- Dirty, scary kitchens
- Trashy smells
- Smells from multiple animals at once
- Pet food covering the sofa
- Pet food covering the floor
- Pet turtle in dirty, smelly water with no food
- Toddler potties left in front of the adult toilet
- No air freshener for the bathroom
- FOUL toilets
- Dirty tubs (i.e. rings, hair, soap stains, etc.)
- Dirty/old shower liners
- Dirty/unchanged bedding with no spare bedding (I had to pull my travel blankets and pillows from the car to sleep ON TOP of the dirty bedding
- Piles of indistinguishable laundry (can't tell if it's dirty or clean) on the floor
- Random dirty clothes (i.e. shirts, socks, pants, etc.) strewn about the house
- Dogs pooping on my intended bedding
- Dog poop in the bathroom (the one I was supposed to use)
- Roaches in the kitchen
- Roaches on the dinet
- Roaches on the floors...OH MY GOD, THE ROACHES!

The horrors I've experienced...! Please, don't let yourself fall guilty of these offenses. And if you have in the past, I won't lie and tell you it's okay because that is NEVER acceptable. Yet since you're reading this, you now have an opportunity to reverse your hosting reputation.

While there is no actual scripture that says "cleanliness is next to godliness," I wholeheartedly believe in it! Where a consistently dirty home is found, you frequently find it connected to poverty, laziness/apathy, or depression. All of these are mindsets, and while I will not in this book, attempt to tackle them, I will say that a person can CHOOSE to reach out for help (which you have if you're reading this book. Kudos!) and CHOOSE to take practical steps to reversing their current situation.

And bear in mind that you don't want to:

1. Make your guests feel uncomfortable by the lack of cleanliness displayed.
2. Make your guests feel obligated to clean YOUR house for whatever reason.
3. Make yourself feel embarrassed over the state of your home.
4. Make your guests feel the need to leave or not stay at your home in the future.
5. Give guests the means by which to gossip about the subpar state of your house.

You (and those who live with you, even if the guests staying are not there at their invitation), should want to keep a clean house, or at least desire to clean it before guests come over.

The "Clean One"

And if you are the "clean one" and you have a spouse, other family member, or roommate who is not, then as awkward and uncomfortable as it may be, at least try to sit them down and have a conversation about changing this in general, and specifically before your guest(s) arrive. And if they live there and are old enough as well as physically able, then they should be helping you clean unless you have some sort of arrangement that precludes their assistance.

You teach people how to treat your house by the way you treat it.

And yes, this includes guests who are merely visiting briefly (e.g. for an afternoon or evening) as well. Make sure all the rooms they may even potentially visit are clean before their arrival.

And yes, this includes the times your family and close friends are your guests as well. This may put them in a particularly awkward position because they want to share with you that they are uncomfortable in your home, yet don't want to risk offending you by telling you the truth. Save them the trouble. Clean up your house.

Chapter 2: Call Pest Control

If you know you have a pest problem—termites, ants, mice, rats, roaches..whatever—then P L E A S E call pest control. This should be a matter of management and maintenance versus scrambling to fix a pest problem, generally speaking. Therefore, you should either hire regular pest control or have your husband, father, or whatever family is most suited to the job (and least likely to spray themselves in the face by accident!) apply the pesticides themself. If you live in an apartment or condo complex, or any other rented home, then the owners will typically handle this unless otherwise stipulated. And anyone is capable of setting out various type of traps and baits for the little buggers.

Localized Pests

Also, the types of pests are likely to vary depending on the state and region you occupy. If you live in Florida or similar regions, lizards are EVERYWHERE, so when it's necessary, be sure to maintain doors, walls, etc. so they will not easily slip into your home. Also, if you live in Florida or California, due to the sheer mass of the populace and never-ending construction, ants are a common issue. And if you have an "ant-attack" every now and then, many times it wasn't due to anything you'd done. This is the same if you live in an area where your neighbors are likely to have roaches. YOU may not be the cause of a nearby infestation, yet you can most certainly avoid them coming in droves to your home by not laying out a red carpet for them. (See Chapter 1.)

Spiders of various poisonous types are frequent visitors to Southern Californians, so please be mindful of this and even give directives if necessary. My former home in California had a planter with a tree in it situated in the far corner of the backyard and in it was a BLACK.WIDOWS'.NEST. #FixItJesus My friends who lived by our high school which was located across town and at the foot of a mountain regularly got TARANTULAS in their backyards. And when I was 17-years-old, I was "sentenced" to do yard work. I was raking up the leaves in my backyard (a safe distance from the aforementioned tree planter) when a BLUISH-PURPLE AND ORANGE FUZZY SPIDER looking as if it belonged to some branch of the tarantula family crawled out of the pile. I didn't say a word. I didn't scream. I maintained my composure, bore my rake in hand, walked into the garage, hung the rake on its appointed hook, and NEVER DID YARD WORK AGAIN. The Lord must've agreed with my resolution (which I never announced to my parents), because I was never asked to do yard work again. *smile*

If you have a genuine pest problem that you are trying without current success to eradicate, then be upfront and honest with your guests as to what MAY occur during their stay. If that is too embarrassing for you (and I wouldn't blame you if it was), then perhaps it would be best to just not host anyone in your home until the problem is well in hand.

Chapter 3: Wash Your Linens

Wash the bedding—especially the sheets!—that your guests will be utilizing during their stay. Change the sheets BEFORE they come, and AFTER they leave. This will make it easier on yourself for the next time guests come to stay in that space. Unless you have a "spare room" reserved for the explicit purpose of housing guests, then this should be a given. You don't want your guests to have to sleep on dirty sheets, nor should you have to sleep on theirs. This is where having spare sheets in stock comes in handy. And this doesn't have to be expensive. You can find attractive, affordable sets at Wal-Mart, Target, T.J. Maxx, and other similar stores.

 If you have tablecloths, placemats, table runners, and the like as well as rugs, then make sure these are clean as well. At least shakeout the rugs.

 And as you're able, replace visibly wearing and out-of-date linens and bedding with newer ones. Some signs of wear and tear include:

- Chews and tears from puppies and cats
- Discolouration from bleach
- Discolouration from sun bleaching
- Various stains (i.e. dirt, blood, cigarettes, pens—the bane of my sheets—etc.)

Also, examine if your pillows and mattresses need to be replaced. The rule of thumb for mattresses is every 8-10 years, while the rule for pillows ranges anywhere from six months to three years, depending on one's cleaning habits, allergies, etc. Yet mattress and pillow protectors will help prolong the life of your items. New mattresses are also meant to be flipped every three months or so.

And if any of your guests will be staying on your air beds, please be sure that they and their attachments are in perfect, working order. Make sure they're not dirty, dusty, or holey. Better yet, blow up the beds for them before they arrive so your guests won't have to fidget with them or make loud noises in the [late] evening.

And if your guests are occupying a room that is generally lived in (e.g. your child's room), then please be sure to remove the dirty laundry from the room or at least keep it out of the way as best you can. Your guests should not have to smell soiled laundry (i.e. workout clothes, sports uniforms, etc.) in their temporary rooms.

Speaking of smells, I'm a huge fan of Febrezing the bedding as I make the bed. After dressing each layer (i.e. mattress protector, fitted sheet, top sheet, etc.), I Febreze, then move on to the next layer.

Chapter 4: Make Room

Set aside clear space for your guests to occupy. Even if it's the sofa, let them know clearly what their space is, and that they are free to get comfortable in it. If they're in a bedroom, then try to set aside space for their clothes in the closet, wardrobe, or dressers, especially if their visit includes professional, church, or wedding-related events.

And give your guests a "sanctified" (set aside) space for them to stay in if at all possible so they won't feel like they're in the way or that their sleeping must be dictated by your comings and goings. Clear out that junky, "catch all" room. Convert your married child's room into a guest room (or at least fix it up a bit if it's too sentimental to redecorate). Renovate your basement, attic, or annex into a spare room. Build a mother-in-law suite or convert that old shed or workshop into a guest space, even a tiny house! (These renovations and conversions will be an excellent selling point should you decide to sell or rent-out your home in the future.) And if you genuinely don't have the space, then try partially converting a den, playroom, or office into a potential, temporary guest room. The furniture you select for that room can play a major role in converting from a den, playroom, or office to a guest room.

Have their sleeping areas made up, and their towels all ready and neatly folded for them. (Preferably a matching or at least colour/pattern-coordinated set. It just looks better, like you put in more thought and effort.) Don't make your guests have to ask for their towels. Simply have them ready.

Chivalry & Respect

If you are a man who does not share a room and you have a woman—any woman—staying over, GIVE.HER.YOUR.ROOM. This is just simple common decency. And if you do it, then chivalry won't be dead. *wink, wink*

And to both genders, if you do not share your room and your parents or other elder family members, friends, etc. are visiting, GIVE.THEM.YOUR.ROOM. Again, this is just showing respect to your elders.

Ladies, if you don't share a room/bed, and if your bed is small and you are not accustomed to or comfortable sharing your bed with your guest or they are not accustomed to or comfortable sharing a bed with you, then GIVE.THEM.YOUR.ROOM.

And yes, if you are sharing your bed with anyone, WASH.YOUR.SHEETS. before they sleep in the bed.

Disclaimer: If you are genuinely not comfortable having a particular person in your bedroom, yet can't avoid having them in your house, feel free to forgo the "Chivalry & Respect" tips, unless, of course, they're your parents, elders in your family. Honour them even if you don't like them.

Finally, regarding "Chivalry & Respect," if you have ladies (or anyone) staying in an open space (e.g. family room) and you have a male guest coming over for any length of time, LET.THEM.KNOW. I recall a time not very long ago that I was knoooocked the heck out on an air mattress in a friend's living room and awoke to her boyfriend sitting in the room. Now ladies, I don't know how *you* dress for sleep, but *I* was NOT.AT.ALL. ready for male company in any way, shape, or form. And as there was no warning whatsoever. I.WAS. LIVID. Not to mention, my hair was A.HOTT.MESS. And I obviously needed to brush my teeth and wash my face.

And to make matters worse, my best friend who was with me and happened to be in the shower earlier, had walked out in a towel as was her custom to find the said boyfriend (admittedly a friend of ours) sitting at the table across from the bathroom. I don't know if she was livid or not, but she was most certainly caught off-guard. I personally woke up to see him catnapping on the table, and was forced to pretend that I was asleep until he left.

Ladies, it's just a matter of simple, common decency to let your female guests know when male company is expected. Take a page from my former college which has, to this day, gender-specific dorms: When a man was on our floor (unless, of course, it was for open house), someone would yell, "Man on the floor!" And we all appreciated the heads up! My friend and I shared this with our younger play-brother, and he is now accustomed to yelling, "Man on the floor!" whenever he walks in the house!

And fellas, these rules are great for your too if you have a guy staying over and a woman is coming over.

Consider how you would feel in such a situation. Consider how your guests would possibly feel and what they might be too uncomfortable to share with you. Do whatever is within your power (and *not* ridiculous) to make your guest(s) as comfortable as possible throughout the duration of their stay.

Chapter 5: Provide Toiletries

Let them know what toiletries you have that they can have access to, or better yet, buy toiletries that are specifically set aside in stock for overnight guests. You can stock up on normal, super, or even travel-sized toiletries depending on your budget, how many people are coming, and how often you host guests or even use the toiletries yourself if you're sharing them. These toiletries may include:

- Toothpaste
- Toothbrushes
- Mouthwash
- Dental floss
- Handsoap
- Body wash
- Bar soap
- Lotion
- Shampoo
- Conditioner
- Combs
- Brushes
- Razors
- Shaving cream
- Feminine products
- Wipes (feminine, make-up, baby, or male)
- Kleenex
- Q-Tips
- Cotton balls
- Shower caps (not just for the ladies!), and so on.

You can also easily procure manicure sets (includes 1 nail file, 2 nail clippers—one larger and one smaller, and 2 orange sticks, and tweezers) at Wal-Mart for $0.97, and Wal-Mart as well as Target, and other grocery stores often have travel-size toiletry sections for very low costs.

Also, be sure to provide towels for your guests. No one should have to travel with a towel unless it's a beach towel or their "sweat cloth" (some singers and preachers will understand this). The standard, *matching* set of towels you should provide for each guest includes:

- One (1) large body towel (consider their body size)
- One (1) largish hair towel (for women and men who have medium-to-long hair and or wash their hair frequently)
- One (1) medium sized towel (great for when guests need to dry their face after washing it)
- One small face towel (washcloth)

There should also be at least one separate towel in the bathroom designated for wiping hands after washing them. And if your guests are staying for approximately two weeks or longer, then make sure that they don't have to ask for a clean set of towels after the first week is up.

Again, you do not have to break the bank to buy towels. The Wal-Mart and Target "ministries" will do just fine. If you prefer, many celebrities carry affordable lines at these stores and others such as Kohl's and you can frequently find name brand towels and other linens at Ross, T.J. Maxx, Marshalls, and HomeGoods. The latter stores are also great places to pick up toiletry sets (e.g. matching hand soap and lotion sets with caddies) as well as designer knick knacks for your bathroom and other spots in your home.

Speaking of knick knacks, this is a great time to speak about space. Take inventory of your:

- Counter space
- Shower/Tub shelf space
- Space for hanging towels/robes

The aforementioned stores are also great to frequent if you need additional shelf space, shower caddies, over-the-door hooks, and so on. And by all means, clean and clear the counter space before your guest arrive and please, put your personal products away after using them if you're sharing a bathroom with your guests. Instruct your other family members/roommates to do so as well if they are sharing bathroom space with your guests.

Providing all of these toiletry-related comforts for your guests, in so much as you are able, is a great consideration since if these things are clearly communicated beforehand, they will not have to travel with some of these items (especially if you use the same brand of products) and thus, will be able to free up space in their luggage for something more important.

Chapter 6: Feed Them

Do your best to have food for your guest(s). Breakfast food, lunch food, dinner food, snack food, all kinds of food. If you're cooking for them, let them know which meals, what times, and what's on the menu. Inquire as to any allergies or aversions they may have. Do your best to not have them feel the need to HAVE to cook for themselves. However, if they are allowed and desire to cook in your home, then let them know what food and drink is at their disposal. This includes the other types of food as well. And be sure to let your cooking guests know whether or not you have a sensitive fire alarm near the kitchen.

Also make them mindful of food that is set aside for various reasons such as:

- Work
- School
- Infants/Toddlers/Children
- Belongs specifically to your roommates/family members
- Medical/Dietary reasons
- Adult beverages

If you have a guest who is addicted to alcohol or prominently abstaining from it, then it would be best to hide away your wine, coffee liqueur, hard cider, rum, gin, etc. in a safe place where they cannot find or reach it. Also, kindly consider this for when you host ministers or Christian laymen who have personal convictions against alcohol. No need to offend your guests or have them viewing you in a certain light because of it. Also, if you host any minors whom you feel might be tempted to dip in the alcohol, then tuck it safely away from them as well.

Kitchen Rules

If you have any particular preferences or rules in place for the kitchen, then please let your guests know in a kindly manner. This may include:

- When/If you run the dishwasher (and if not, if they're allowed to)
- If you prefer the sink(s) to be kept empty, and when or by what time (e.g. we clear the sink at night)
- Whether or not you want them to clean up after themselves, or if you, a child with chores, or a maid, etc. will do it for them
- If they're allowed to eat/drink in their room or any other rooms around the house

Setting these clear boundaries will also assist you in keeping any (female) guests who may feel inclined to unnecessarily and erroneously dictate the running of *your* kitchen to you in their proper place.

Chapter 7: Provide a Peaceful Atmosphere

As much as is within your power, provide your guests with a peaceful environment. No loud music, loud talking, loud T.V. or movies, unless, of course, you are all enjoying each others' company and in agreement that this is the time and place for it.

Be mindful of your guests' sleep schedules, especially if they are or have children/youths or elderly guests travelling with them, or have particularly early wake-up calls. While most of us simply set our alarms on our phones, if you can provide them with an alarm clock, this is a great option should they want to turn off or silence their phones at any time.

Providing your guests with the aforementioned "sanctified space" will also help to cut down on the concern for them experiencing loud noises, including infants, toddlers, and children. This also applies if you have an uninsulated music room (officially or unofficially). However, if at all possible, the loud practicing (singing or playing) should be kept to a minimum out of respect for your guests for the duration of their stay.

Also, remember that Chapter 1 will contribute to the feel of a peaceful environment. Mess = chaos.

Chapter 8: Maintain a Fragrant Environment

If you're home frequently, step outside and step back in to see if there is an odor associated with your home. Is it food? Is it *spoiled* food? Is it that trash that needs to be taken out? Do a onceover your whole house to make sure that there are no awkward or bad smells in your home. Utilize air and fabric Febreze as well as carpet deodorizers. If your carpet is beyond fabric Febreze and deodorizers (or stained), then shampoo the carpet. You can hire someone to do it for you or if you have a Food Lion nearby, you can rent your own shampooer as well as the shampoo to put in it. You'll need a little muscle and coordination if there are rugs involved, but it can be done.

    Maintaining a fragrant environment includes your air conditioners. Make sure they are not blowing mold or blue/black fragments into the air. (You'll notice the black or blue fragments if the dust around your home isn't the generic white or grey.) If there is a mold problem, call your AC/Vac company or maintenance at your rental property to handle the problem. And this is just something good to do because NOBODY wants mold in their home. Just read the Old Testament!

    And PLEASE provide smell-good products around your home for the comfort of your guests and yourselves. These may include:

- Timed air fresheners
- Plug-in air fresheners
- Febreze or Glade sprays in the bathrooms (Febreze is silent *wink, wink*)
- Candles
- Fragrance sticks
- Fragrance beads
- Fragrant oils/waxes, etc.

All of this is especially important if you have pets, which leads me to my next point...

Chapter 9: Control Your Pets...And Theirs

First of all, if you have pets, clearly communicate this to your guests. If they have a fear of big dogs or are allergic to cats and you have them, and if other accommodations for you pets cannot or will not be made, then perhaps you would not be the best host for this particular guest. Second, make sure your home doesn't smell like dog/cat/fish, etc. There are Fabric Fresheners for this explicit purpose by Febreze and other brands. Make sure unsavoury discoveries are not strewn or hiding around the house. And if your pet sheds like my dog does, then you'll want to do a thorough sweep and vacuuming of the floors as well as checking the furniture and bedding depending on what furniture your pets are allowed on (and climb on even if they're not allowed). Also, if your dogs are chewers or your cats are scratchers, then do your best to check and repair any damaged furniture, etc.

    Also, keep your pet(s) in check. If they are outdoor dogs and properly fenced in the backyard, then this should be a relatively simple problem. If you have indoor dogs, then you best would know how to introduce your pet to your guests. For my dog, Smokey, we generally keep him in "his" room (the laundry room) or a bedroom so he can bark his head off, and once he's calmed down, we can better introduce him to the guest. And if it is someone he is familiar with like a visiting/returning family member, then we know to let him out back and introduce the person to him there because Miniature

Schnauzers (or at least ours) are prone to pee a bit when they're excited.

Ultimately, you know your pet and what they're prone to do on a given basis, so make this known as is necessary to your guests, and keep them in hand as much as is needed. You don't want your guests to feel that your pet is more important to you than they are (even if it's true!).

Furthermore, if your guests have pets, please let them know:

1. If bringing pets is acceptable.
2. If it is, what precautions they should take.
3. What the house rules are.

You WILL have to discuss house rules (see Chapter 12), and also have to put your heads together so as to introduce your pets to each other if you have them. You'll also need to let them know your condo or Homeowners' Association's rules for dog walkers if applicable.

Chapter 10: Coordinate Your Schedules

We're all busy these days, so unless your guests have come for vacation and even if they have, it is important to at the very least discuss your projected schedules, if not coordinate them. This is particularly important if you are not providing your guests with a spare key, which is, of course, preferable, unless you have keypad entry which is wonderfully convenient for you as well as your guests.

You should both be mindful of scheduling factors such as:

- Work hours
- (Children's) school hours
- Church hours
- Engagements away from home
- Engagements at home
- Whether or not your guests are invited/expected at your various engagements

Make sure your guests' plans as well as yours—including your hopes for this particular trip—are clearly expressed and clearly understood.

Disclaimer: Do not, I repeat—DO NOT—manipulate your guests into staying with you OR spending time with you. As aforementioned, people have their own plans—especially if they are grown—and while it is fine for you to communicate your desires for your guests while on this trip, it is not acceptable, friendly, nor fair to place manipulative conditions upon their stay such as "You can only stay with me if you hang out with me." Manipulation is witchcraft (I had to get deep at SOME point! I'm a biblical teacher!), and if they are your loved one—and if if they're not—you don't want to be guilty (innocently or otherwise) of operating in that spirit or inflicting it upon others.

People can get REAL funny when you're in their space. Don't be that person. Be the host/hostess that makes your guests WANT to come back (within reason) and have a good feeling after they've left.

Chapter 11: Provide a List of Nearby Necessities, Food & Fun

If your guests are not familiar with the area, it would be nice to provide them with a list of nearby necessity stops and places of entertainment, just like the hotels do. List items such as:

- Gas stations
- Grocery stores
- Drug stores
- Cleaners
- Restaurants (fast food and sit-down)
- Malls/Outlets
- Movie theaters
- Theme parks
- Gyms
- Parks
- Walking trails
- Dog(friendly) parks, etc.

Also, remember: GPS is one thing, but personal recommendations are quite another. Word-of-mouth testimonials are awesome because they're free marketing with the built-in testimonial factor from someone they trust: you.

Chapter 12: Clearly Communicate

This is a wonderful list if I do say so myself, but it means nothing if your expectations are not clearly communicated. Here are some items that should be discussed and or clearly communicated to your guests:

- Length of stay*
- When they're expected to arrive
- Your wake-up time
- Your bedtime
- Your children's naptimes and bedtime(s)
- Your elderly family member's wake-up time
- Your elderly family member's bedtime
- Maid's schedule
- Nanny's schedule
- Schedules of any other personal assistants, associates, etc. who work or have access to your home
- Anticipated deliveries
- Lawn service schedule
- Gate codes (gated communities and complexes)
- Alarm codes & when they're set as well as when/if they go off
- Preferred or enforced curfews (should your guests be home by a certain time, hopefully not for adults)
- Contact numbers
- Wi-Fi username & password
- Kitchen rules
- Whether or not alcohol is allowed
- Whether or not smoking/tobacco is allowed and if yes, where (e.g. outside)

- Lights you generally leave on or dimmed while gone or at night
- Acceptable parking**
- Dog walking rules
- Whether or not your guests' guests are allowed; if yes, visiting times
- Any quirks/pet peeves pertaining to the house, electronics (i.e. T.V., DVD players, home theaters, game consoles, universal remotes, etc.), the property itself, ringing doorbells, etc.

*If your guests are long-term guests, in so much as it is possible, clearly communicate your expectation of duration (i.e. one month max, two months, until the baby comes, after the baby comes, etc.). If relevant and necessary, inquire as to how long they are in need of staying. And revisit this topic as cordially as possible with your guest(s) if necessary, finding a happy medium between not vexing them and not allowing them to permanently move in (unless you want them to or are compelled to).

**Let your guests know whether or not they're allowed to:

- Park in the garage and if yes, on what side?
- Park in the driveway and if yes, on what side?
- Park in the street and if yes, on what side?
- Park under covered vs. uncovered parking (e.g. for complexes)? If yes, what number(s)?
- Park for free? paid? valet?

This is probably also a good time to let them know if you are allowing them the use of your car(s), and if yes, which one(s)?

And don't forget to provide them with the spare key/key code as well as instructions on the type of gas required and any related quirks they should know about.

The ultimate goal of good hosting is to make your guests feel all the comforts of (a) home without any of the responsibilities and pressures of home. Treat them special, even if they are frequent visitors. Hospitality was a massive deal in the Ancient World, and even today, it plays as major role whether you are hosting friends or guest speakers for your church or organization's event. Use this as your opportunity to pour peace and comfort into someone, either directly or otherwise.

Bonus: How to Set Up a Guest Room

This bonus chapter will take the various topics we've previously discussed and compile them to create a lovely, comfortable "spare room" for your guests to enjoy.

The Guest Room

Make Room

Everyone does not have the space to create a separate room for their overnight guests, and that's okay. However, if you do not have a current room designated for guests, consider implementing one or some of the following actions:

1. Redecorate your adult child's bedroom (if they don't still live at home).
2. Tweak or upgrade your adult child's bedroom. (This is great if you'd like to maintain the feel of the room, but simply want to update and "grow up" some aspects for guests.)
3. Redecorate your husband's man cave (but only if he agrees first!).
4. Clean out your "catch all" room.
5. Clean out your attic (if it's safe to sleep in!).
6. Let your office double as a guest room. ("Hideaway" furniture is great for this concept.)

7. Carve out a corner in your den or child(ren)'s playroom.

All of these are great options that can be either upgraded, redecorated, or fully renovated depending on your budget. And if all of your rooms are truly occupied, you may keep these ideas we're about to discuss in mind for when you have to temporarily commandeer one of your children's bedrooms and make it comfortable for your guests. But for those who have a spare room, let's break down how to set it up for your guests.

Make the Bed
Find a Bed or Beds

Find a bed that will be suitable for your guests. Depending on your budget, availability, and plans, decided whether or not you'd like a California king, king, queen, full, or twin-sized bed. You may also have the options of:

1. Twin beds (plural)
2. Bunk beds (especially great for kids)
3. Trundle beds (also great for kids)
4. Sleeper sofas
5. Sleeper loveseats
6. Sleeper Chairs
7. Traditional sofas/Sectionals/Loveseats/Chaises

And if you are in the process of setting up your guest room, but your visitors have beat you to it, you can at least place a decent-sized air mattress in it and make it up comfortably for your guests until you can bring in the furniture of your choosing. There are several options. Simply choose what's best for your current situation.

Prepare the Linens

If you already have a lovely bedding set put aside, great! If not, feel free to shop around for one at places such as Wal-Mart; Target; T.J. Maxx; Marshalls; Home Goods; Ross; Kohl's; Bed, Bath & Beyond; or any other department store or boutique of your choosing. Whatever you select, make sure the bedding is coordinated—sheets, pillowcases, pillows, comforters, duvets, throws, etc. You don't want your guests sleeping on mismatched sheets. You might not mind or notice, but they might!

And, of course, wash all bedding before using it. Be sure to use fabric softener (if you like) and dryer sheets. Also, a little trick I love to implement when making a bed is to Febreze as I go. Preferably with fabric Febreze, but also with regular Febreze (or Glade, or Air Wick, etc.) depending on what's available. I lightly Febreze each layer: the fitted sheet, the loose sheet, the comforter, and the pillowcases (both sides). It's just an extra touch that's easily done to make your guest's experience that much better.

You may also consider allowing your sheets to tumble in the dryer and knock out some of those folds and wrinkles they've developed from sitting in the linen closet, or even iron them if you are so inclined.

Jazz It Up

If you're tired of your current bedding that you were previously used, this is a great time to hit one of the many cost-efficient stores mentioned in the last section, and purchase a new bedding set. If you have twin, bunk, or trundle beds in your guest room, then you may either purchase matching sets or complimentary sets such as:

- Stripes & Flowers/Damask
- Stripes & Plaids
- Stripes & Shapes
- Stripes & Other Design
- Same Pattern, Complimentary Colours
- Complimentary Pattern, Same Colours
- Coordinated Themes (i.e. birds and butterflies, ballerinas and bows, anchors and boats, maps and globes, etc.)

Find some fun throw pillows that are adhere to your bedding's theme and or colour scheme(s). Or if you can't buy them, consider sewing some pillow cases. You may even sew a fitted duvet or quilt (or commission someone to) for your new bedding look.

If you're not sure or not daring enough, head to Pinterest.com or even just a plain old fashioned Google image search for some bedding ideas.

And finally, tweak and switch up the bedding, throw pillows, throw blankets, etc. to reflect the seasons.

Provide a Nightstand

Whether it's a formal nightstand, a conveniently placed bookshelf, a chair or stool, or a lamp that doubles as a nightstand, find something that will serve as a nightstand for your guests. And if possible, make sure there's an outlet nearby. Everyone hates having to walk across the room to charge their phone overnight.

Let There Be Light

How's the lighting in your guest room? If it's already great, then fine. However, if it's still too dim, consider adding a floor lamp, a lamp on the nightstand, a nightlight, or a better light fixture (preferably with a fan) to the ceiling. Also be sure to check the lighting in the [walk-in] closet if there is one as well as the bathroom they'll be using as well.

In turn, you'll want to check the room to make sure that at night and even in the morning, the light coming through the curtains or blinds is sufficiently blocked out.

Provide Storage

Make sure there is sufficient space in the closet(s), wardrobe(s), and or dresser(s) so your guests may comfortably store their clothes and other items throughout the duration of their stay. Even better if they can stow away their luggage for a particularly lengthy stay. Also take into consideration the furniture and floor space to make sure they have the necessary space for luggage on the floor, especially for guests stay shorter periods of time or who do not have as much space (or desire) to unpack.

Mind the Seasons

Take note of the season and projected weather conditions. How do they affect the interior atmosphere of your home? For all weather conditions, a good rule of thumb is to make note of the comments and actions of people who visit your home. Do they generally say things like, "It's an ice box in here!" or "It's stifling in here!" Do they prefer to keep their coats on or a blanket around them, or do they start stripping down excessively? Be mindful of even someone's unconscious behaviour. A temperature that's comfortable for you may be darn near unbearable for someone else with a different internal temperature or preference.

Also note that heat may make some things in your trash can smell more than they typically would at other times, so be particularly mindful of seeing to your trash before guests arrive. If you're struck with the urge to clean out your fridge the night before guests come (which is admirable and necessary!), make sure to take the trash to wherever you keep your trash cans out of doors. That said, here are some seasonal and temperature-specific items to see to.

Warm Weather

- Make sure your home's temperature is comfortably cool without being an icebox.
    - If you have an extenuating circumstance like pregnancy or menopause and you need your

temperature to remain extremely cool indoors, then please make sure to provide extra blankets and so forth for your guests, not to mention the other members of your household.
- Be mindful that bugs and other undesirables are more active around and in your house when it's warm outside.
    - Make sure there are no bee, hornet, wasp, yellow-jacket, mudbugger, etc. nests near the entryways of your home that guests would frequently use. Also be mindful if those said nests are near windows.
        - Do your windows have a screen?
        - Does the screen keep the insects out?
    - Do you have a nest or an infestation? If it's an infestation, call your local exterminator or other person qualified to deal with such a matter.
        - If you have an inconvenient bee colony near your entryway(s) or any place on your property, please be mindful that bees are officially endangered as of this year (2017), and an extremely necessary part of our eco-system. So call your local beekeeper or anyone else qualified to deal with this situation who can safely remove the colony, save the bees, and and restore comfort to your living situation.
- If there is a local infestation in your neighborhood, city, etc. (e.g. I have a host of large spiders in various types in my currently neighborhood and not much can be done about them), be sure to warn your guests as best you can without alarming them too much.

- Make sure there are fans in the guest rooms; if not on the ceiling, then be sure to get a fan to place in the room the guests will be staying in.
- Let your guests know whether or not they can (or are allowed to) open the windows, and if there are any quirks or alarms attached to them. (I once set off a home's alarm by opening a bathroom window after a shower! Talk about embarrassing!)
- If you have flannel sheets or extremely thick blankets on the bed your guest(s) will be staying in, be sure to switch them out for something a little more cool and lightweight, unless of course they prefer the warmer linens.
- If you have a pool or body of water nearby, and there are any instructions to accompany it, then please make those known to your guests if applicable.
  - If your guests don't know you have a pool, jacuzzi, etc., let them know before they arrive.
  - If your guests do know you have a pool, jacuzzi, etc., but it won't be operable at the time of their visit, then let them know that.
  - If there is a community pool, make your guests abreast of the times and any applicable unique rules.
  - Warn guests of any water-related predators such as sharks, alligators, snakes, etc. that may be temporarily or permanently frequenting the respective bodies of water.
  - If at all possible, provide your guests with beach towels so they don't have to bring their own. Let the guests know where they can find them, or leave them in a convenient place for them to

find. These can be easily found at Wal-Mart, Target, Home Goods, T.J. Maxx, Ross, etc.

Changing Weather

If it's Spring or Fall [in a place with four seasons] or you live somewhere with temperamental weather (e.g. sunny one moment, a deluge the next) or where the drastic temperature changes between morning and afternoon or evening, then these items may apply to you.

- Provide a fan if one is not already located in the room. They may not need it at night, but possibly during the morning and day.
- Provide additional blankets at the end of the bed, corner chair, or somewhere easily accessible for your guests.
- Keep an eye on the home temperature. You may need to heighten or lower it depending on what the weather does and how that affects your home's interior temperature.
- If you have extra umbrellas your guests may need, let them know where they can find them or situate them somewhere in the guest room.
- If your guest is bringing a dog (or other pet that ventures outdoors) and it's going to be rainy or snowy, then make sure your guests have means by which to clean the paws (and body) of the pet so your floors and linens are kept clean.
- Be mindful that with changing weather, critters that typically live out of doors may try to find shelter in your home.

Cold Weather

- Provide additional blankets for your guests just in case they're needed.
- If you have floors that get particularly cold (i.e. wood, tile, concrete, etc.), then do your best to provide a rug near the bed, in front of the bathroom sink, hallway, and anywhere else they may need it.
- If there is a fireplace in your guest quarters, let your guests know how it works, if it is operable, and where to find the necessary items (i.e. switch, wood, etc.) to operate it.
- If you don't have a real fireplace in your guests' room, you consider providing a faux fireplace or heater if necessary or desired.
- Make sure your out-of-town guests know just how cold the weather gets where you live, if the weather is uncharacteristic or unseasonably cold, and what sort of coat is appropriate, especially if they're from somewhere with extremely warm or tropical temperatures.

Another great way of looking out for our guests is giving them a head's up on the extended forecast throughout the duration of their stay.

The Bathroom

A clean room is wonderful, but a subpar bathroom can ruin your guest's whole vibe. Naturally, a person wants the room in which they go to *get* clean to already *be* clean. Also, bear in mind that your guest may have a long, packed schedule during their visit or a not-so-pleasant reason for visiting. A clean, serene bathroom will help just that much to ease their burden, if only a little bit. So with that in mind, here are some pointers to provide a better visiting experience for your guest.

Clean the Bathroom

This should be understood, but let's state it just in case: clean whatever bathroom your guests will be using *en totale*. Sink, tub/shower, toilet, floors, etc. If you have small children that typically use that particular bathroom, perhaps let them use yours or at least a different one during your guest's stay. Even if the bathroom is generally thought to be clean, check for the following:

- **Dirty toilet bowl.** Even if a bathroom is unused, toilet bowls always have a way of becoming filthy from disuse.
- **Dust.** Just run a feather duster or cloth over the surfaces to make sure all is dust-free.
- **Mildew/Mold.** Due to the nature of bathrooms and humid environments if you live in them, it can be easy for mold of various types to grow in bathrooms. To prevent this, try to keep your bathroom well ventilated, using a fan during showers, etc. Air them out if needed. To deal with mold, google *how to remove mold* if it looks like a manageable problem. If it's a larger problem, call someone who specializes in this to deal with the problem. If you live in an apartment, condo, or anywhere else where repairs are included in the rent, then call the designated person so they can send the appropriate person to deal with the problem.

- **Floors.** Even if a floor looks clean, it's amazing the things your feet feel once you've stepped out of the shower! Checking the floors includes checking the rugs on the floors. Shake or beat them out; wash them if necessary. Nobody wants to feel like they're back in college and *have* to wear shower shoes in your bathroom.
- **Trash.** Make sure to dump the trash can before any guests arrive.
- **Fragrance.** Always keep Febreze or some other such air freshener easily accessible in the bathroom for your guests. And go the extra mile to keep it smelling fresh 24/7 with items such as:
    - Timed or motion-detecting air fresheners
    - Oil diffuser plugins
    - Fragrant wax plugins
    - Potpourri
    - Candles
    - (Be mindful of whether or not there are small children who may burn themselves on the fire, wax, oil, etc. or attempt to eat the potpourri.)

Provide Linens

Make up the bed as best and beautifully as you can. Select a sheet set that is not only complimentary colour-wise, but also pattern-wise to the cover you are using. The sheet set should have:

- A fitted sheet
- A top sheet
- 1-2 matching pillow cases depending on the sheet size*

*If there are more pillows than cases in the set, utilize any other pillow cases you have or can find that are complimentary to the colour and pattern schemes, even if they are not matchy-matchy.

For the top cover, a comforter, substantial blanket, or duvet is acceptable. If you decide to use a duvet, make sure that there is either a complimentary comforter or blanket to go under it if the duvet is thin and completely separate or a comforter to go inside it if it is the type of duvet that is meant to be the case for a comporter.

If you are providing air beds, trundle beds, or even sofas, etc. for your guests to sleep on, then be sure to be mindful of how many blankets they'll need, and whether or not it would be more comfortable for them to have a layer to sleep on if they are on the air bed or sofa.

And as always, provide the necessary grouping of towels *before your guests arrive* as discussed in Chapter 5 for each of your guests. You may place these on their bed or on the bathroom counter, etc.; somewhere they can easily find them.

Think Ahead

All in all, just think ahead. Think about your guests, their way of life, any difficulties or disabilities they may have, and do your best to consider them. Here are some examples:

- If you have upstairs and downstairs guest rooms available, then consider placing your elderly, (heavily) pregnant, injured, or physically disabled guests in the

- downstairs room so they won't have to toil in climbing up and down stairs.
- If you have a home theater, family room, den, or playroom from which loud noises generally emanate at inconvenient times, try to not situate guests near those spots. Or consider lowering the noise level when guests are staying with you, unless, of course, they're happy to make noise with you!
- If you have a family with small children staying with you and they are not all staying in the same room, consider having the children stay in as close proximity to their parents as possible.
- If you have, for example, your grandmother and nephew or niece staying with you at the same time and you only have one guest bed, practice consideration and respect by giving the bed to your grandmother, and placing the niece or nephew on your sofa, air bed, etc.

Consider Your Children

On a darker, more serious note, be mindful of your children, wife, or any other potentially physically vulnerable people who live with you or who will be staying with you at the time any other guests are. If your wife, child, etc. is uncomfortable around that guest, be mindful. If you're able to, find out why. Perhaps this is someone who does not need access to your home, at least overnight. If it can't be avoided, take additional precautions to maintaining the safety of your home above all else.

Follow your gut.

If you don't want your father, brother, uncle, grandfather, etc. sleeping near your child, don't let them. Keep your child in your room if necessary. The safety of your child should be your number one priority. And sadly, there are female predators too, even though society still scoffs at it. If there are questionable female characters staying in your home, and it cannot be avoided, then look to your young [minor] son (or daughter).

"Most children are abused by someone they know and trust, according to the American Psychological Association. An estimated 60% of perpetrators are known to the child but not family members: family friends, babysitters, child care providers and neighbors," (CNN).

Sharon Doty, the founder of the Empowering Adults—Protecting Children non-profit organization, gives these tips for preventing abuse to your children. Look out for:

- **People who want to be alone with children:** If a predator has nurtured a relationship, you may be inclined to let him or her be alone with your child if the adult asks. But just say no.
- **People who break the parents' rules:** Be wary of people who give your children candy or food against your wishes or let your child do things you don't allow them to do. "It creates a secret relationship. You have to be advocate for no secrets by teaching that it's never OK for someone to ask them to keep something from a parent."

Doty provided CNN with some warning signs of children and teens who've been abused:

- Adopting unusual behaviours
- Dressing shabbily to make themselves less attractive/appealing
- Withdrawing or isolating themselves
- New symptoms of depression or anxiety
- Poor performance in school
- Disinterest in activities they used to enjoy
- Sudden dislike for a teacher or coach, etc.
- Substance abuse
- Mood swings
- Changes in eating habits
- Adult-like sex behaviours

Doty also insists: "Listen to your gut."

And men especially, if your wife or another trustworthy woman in your life (especially one who is a good judge of character) tells you they are uncomfortable with someone being in your home—either around your children or them—LISTEN. Better safe than sorry.

Here are two real-life examples of following your gut:

Example #1: In my own life, there was a family member I was never, and I do mean NEVER, comfortable around. I never ever ever wanted to be around him and to this day, I feel the same way. As I small child, I remember several of out-of-state family members surprising us for a visit. One of them was hiding behind our fence gate. (It was tall enough to hide a grown man.) When we opened the gate and saw who it was, I was genuinely displeased that it was him.

 Years later in college, another female family member of mine said that she had to go on a long road trip with this family member and she felt *so* uncomfortable with him. She was concerned for her bodily safety in a sexual sense. Now there is no record to our knowledge of this family member ever sexually abusing anyone inside of our family or out, yet there was one brief outburst years ago—long before I was born—of physical violence against a female family member. He snapped and came to before he did any extensive damage, but the fact is that he did it.

Example #2: I have a friend who is married with a beautiful little girl. When her father-in-law comes over, he makes comments about wanting to sleep in her daughter's room and she is adamantly against it. She too has heard no record of this man man ever sexually or otherwise abusing anyone, yet she is a woman and a mother, and she knows when something is not right.

 I would venture to say that the difference between many a potential molester/abuser and an actual molester/abuser is opportunity; the perfect storm. There are men [and women] who may fantasize about raping women or molesting children, but have never crossed that line for whatever reason. You can help protect yourself and your children by not providing those individuals with the opportunity.

 FOLLOW YOUR GUT.

Now that that unpleasant topic is out of the way, I hope that in every way, this small book has given you practical tips to ready your home for overnight guests in a way that considers them as well as the peace of your home. Make your home welcoming, just remember that you do not have to welcome everyone into it, and certainly not overnight. Happy hosting!

Contact

DesireeMMondesir.com (primary)
Blogpreneur.us
TheHostessList.wordpress.com
DAWeddings.wordpress.com
WriteWaytoLight.wordpress.com

Facebook: @DesireeMMondesir
Instagram: @DesireeMMondesir
Twitter: @DesireeMondesir

Made in the USA
Coppell, TX
07 November 2020